THE DAVID SERIES #2

A TALE OF TWO BROTHERS

From Rivalry to Friendship

Retold by
Dr. Veronika Amaku

Illustrated by
Hakuya ID

Ambassador Publishing
RAISING FOUNDATIONS OF MANY GENERATIONS

Copyright © 2024 by Veronika Amaku

Published in 2024 by Ambassador Publishing. All rights reserved. No part of this book may be used or reproduced in any manner whatsoever without written permission except in the case of brief quotations embodied in critical articles and reviews.

Scripture quotations are taken from the Holy Bible, New Living Translation, copyright ©1996, 2004, 2015 by Tyndale House Foundation. Used by permission of Tyndale House Publishers, Carol Stream, Illinois 60188. All rights reserved.

Art Direction and Book Design by Toluwanimi Babarinde

Illustrations by Hakuya ID

Send inquiries to ambassador.publish@gmail.com

Hardcover ISBN: 978-0-9788390-3-1

Paperback ISBN: 978-0-9788390-4-8

Published in the United States of America

For Young Readers

My goal is to inspire young readers through relatable, captivating stories highlighting David's courage, perseverance, failures, and faith.

The family was very close, and the kids probably helped each other with their chores. At night, they may sit by the campfire and listen to stories.

Imagine the troubled look on the faces of the town folks when they saw Samuel! "Is everything well," the elders asked as they met with him. "Did you arrive peacefully?"

Samuel, smiling, calmly replied, "Of course, I come in peace." "I came to pray to God. Please invite Jesse and his sons."

When Jesse arrived, he presented his sons to Samuel. When Samuel saw Eliab's heroic appearance, he concluded, "Surely this is the Lord's anointed!" But the Lord admonished Samuel, "Don't judge a man by his appearance or height, though. I have rejected him," the Lord said.

The Lord does not view things in the same manner that humans do. While people judge based on appearance, the Lord considers the heart.

Then each time Jesse presented all his other sons except David to Samuel, Samuel said no. None were chosen by the Lord.

Finally, after Samuel asked if he had any more sons, Jesse brought David.

As soon as David walked in, God told Samuel, "This is the one; anoint him!" Samuel anointed little David with a special oil to be the next king in front of his big brothers and the rest of the family!

After some time, there was war in the land. The Philistines, led by the warrior, Goliath, tried to take over the Istaelite's land. Goliath was a really, really big guy! He had a huge spear and was decked out in heavy bronze armor that made him look even more scary!

David volunteered to fight against Goliath and God helped him. David defeated the giant with his sling just like he did to the lions and the bears!

The women and children had a street parade as they sang and danced in honor of David.

Even Eliab picked up a valuable lesson that day. He realized that God was with David and he needed to support and love his brother no matter what.

Eliab became one of David's powerful helpers who assisted him as king.

LESSONS LEARNED:

1. What is the condition of your heart?

God rejected Eliab because of what was on his heart, but God saw David's heart that he desired to do the right thing.

James 4:6-8 says, "God opposes the proud but gives grace to the humble... Come close to God, and God will come close to you."

2. David was an ordinary kid who did extraordinary things.

You can be that kid too. Since he faithfully cared and risked his life for the animals, God knew that David would do the same for his people. From being a good shepherd boy, God chose him to be king! "Whatever you do, do well." Ecclesiastes 9:10.

3. Don't look down on others.

Don't think that others cannot be good enough. Prophet Samuel made the mistake of only looking at Eliab's physical build. He almost selected the wrong king!

Even Jesse, their dad, did not consider David as a probable choice! He brought all the other boys to Samuel but not David!

Jesus was twelve years old when he was in the temple teaching the old teachers! Be encouraged like Paul did to Timothy, when he said, "Don't allow anyone to despise your youth." Yes, you too can be used by God!

5. Family is very important.

When Eliab didn't get picked as king, he might have felt surprised and/or jealous. The way he queried David when he brought food supplies could either be because he really cared about David, he did not want him to get hurt on the battlefield, or he felt that David was arrogant since he was going to be king.

Even though he might have had a mix of emotions at first, as time went by, Eliab knew that being family was more important. He later helped David a lot and was one of David's trusted supporters.

THE END

About the author

Dr. Veronika Amaku

Dr. Veronika Amaku, a devoted wife, mother, and college professor, inspires through unwavering faith.

Born again in 1983, she actively served in campus Christian organizations and as a trained worker with Children Evangelism Ministry. She nurtured young minds with the wisdom of the Bible by teaching Sunday schools and establishing Bible Clubs for children in Nigeria and the United States.

Guided by God's grace, she raised five children who love the Lord. Her life exemplifies faith's transformative power. Her children's books impart values of love, faith, and compassion, touching young hearts worldwide.

She is a remarkable author and role model.

About the series

The David Series is a collection of children's books that feature the biblical David as the protagonist.

The goal is to inspire young readers through relatable, captivating stories highlighting David's courage, perseverance, failures, and faith.

To keep children engaged, we incorporated an art style that is highly adept at evoking emotions and bridging the gap between classic and modern tales.

Furthermore, the illustrations' inclusive nature promote diversity and expose youngsters to different artistic styles and cultures, cultivating a deep appreciation for the arts.

Heartfelt Appreciation

Words can barely describe my immense gratitude toward everyone who has been a part of this remarkable journey. Bringing this book from thought to life has been a group effort filled with passion, creativity, and tireless dedication.

I give the glory to God for the inspiration and guidance toward making this book a reality. I pray that this book brings faith and life to readers across the globe.

Dr. Toluwanimi Babarinde, you have been the backbone of this project, and your contributions have been invaluable.

Hakuya ID, you are a gem. You breathed life into our characters with your anime-style artistry. You captured the story's essence and added a unique charm that will surely captivate our young readers.

Dr. Innocent Ononiwu, you paid meticulous attention to detail as a reviewer, and, despite your busy schedule, you spent hours refining each page.

Thank you for your dedication to excellence.

Lastly, thanks to my husband, Dr. Samuel Amaku, whose belief in my potential has been a great source of encouragement, and to my children, Josh, Ruth, Grace, Esther, and Mary, whose confidence in this project has been a constant source of strength for me. My siblings, their families, and friends, I am grateful for your endless support, encouragement, prayers, and inspiration.

Together, we have created something that will continue to raise the foundations of many generations for eternity, even after we go Home. This book is not merely a product of ink and paper but a God-inspired expression of our collective creativity, passion, and determination.

With heartfelt thanks,
Dr. Veronika Amaku
Ambassador Publishing

www.ingramcontent.com/pod-product-compliance
Lightning Source LLC
Chambersburg PA
CBHW061815290426
44110CB00026B/2881